SIX SESSIO
STUDY GUIDE

THE
BEAUTIFUL
UGLY
TRUTH

REBUILDING TRUST AFTER BETRAYAL

GWEN BRAGUE

Published by Two Penny Publishing
850 E Lime Street #266
Tarpon Springs, FL 34688
TwoPennyPublishing.com
info@twopennypublishing.com

For permission requests and ordering information, email the publisher at:
info@twopennypublishing.com

Scripture quotations marked (ESV) are from The ESV® Bible (The Holy Bible, English Standard Version®), copyright © 2001 by Crossway, a publishing ministry of Good News Publishers. Used by permission. All rights reserved."

Scripture quotations marked (MSG) are taken from The Message, copyright © 1993, 2002, 2018 by Eugene H. Peterson. Used by permission of NavPress. All rights reserved. Represented by Tyndale House Publishers.

Scripture quotations marked (TPT) are from The Passion Translation®. Copyright © 2017, 2018, 2020 by Passion & Fire Ministries, Inc. Used by permission. All rights reserved. ThePassionTranslation.com.

ISBN: 978-1-950995-82-0

FIRST EDITION

For more information about the author or to book her for your next event or media interview, please contact her representative at: info@twopennypublishing.com

Two Penny Publishing is a partnership publisher of a variety of genres. We help first-time and seasoned authors share their stories, passion, knowledge, and experiences that help others grow and learn. Please visit our website: TwoPennyPublishing.com if you would like us to consider your manuscript or book idea for publishing.

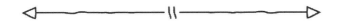

"But God's not finished. He's waiting around to be *gracious* to you."

Isaiah 30:18a (MSG)

Table of Contents

Foreword

My name is Mark. I am the husband and Pastor referred to in "The Beautiful Ugly Truth."

The Study Guide you are preparing to read is a companion to the book "The Beautiful Ugly Truth." It is a very honest and transparent look into the most transformative time in our life and marriage. Some of it may be tough to read because of Gwen's honesty. Her stripped down, raw description of her emotion in the moments of the pain and the hurt my actions caused her may cause you some discomfort.

It might remind you of some painful moments in your own life.

It may be a picture of what you are walking through even now.

You may find yourself triggered by her honesty.

Don't look for fluff here.

In "The Beautiful Ugly Truth" you hear how Gwen walked in forgiveness for me when I did not deserve it and she did not feel like it.

You feel Gwen's pain when she learned the truth of my involvement in pornography.

Funny thing about the truth is that you have heard it sets us free. The reality is, more often than not, the truth hits the fan first and makes a mess of the tidy life you thought you had…and then it sets you free.

In "The Beautiful Ugly Truth" you hear how Gwen's obedience to God in those messy, truth-hitting-the-fan moments opened the door for my healing.

The Beautiful Ugly Truth Study Guide companion will give you tools and a road map through which you can begin to build trust in your own situation.

People have asked us how we can be so transparent with our story. We have been asked how we find the courage to do so.

The Word tells us how we are made overcomers by the Blood of the Lamb and the word of our testimony. The blood is something Jesus did. It is a constant and it remains true... no matter what.

The variable is the word of our testimony. Our testimony is our story. The Word of our testimony is quite simply the telling of our story and how it glorifies God. So, every time we tell our story, we glorify what God has done and we are made more of an overcomer.

That is why we tell our story. The good, the bad, the ugly, the beautiful. It makes us overcomers.

What gives us confidence to continue to tell it is the way in which people from all walks of life respond and share a similar hurt or pain.

As we tell our story, we find ourselves in conversation after conversation, which allow us to witness the most effective life changing ministry moments we have ever experienced in our lives.

And the best part? We know it is nothing we did. It is not a slick message. It is not a cool turn of phrase or clever alliteration.

It is the grace of God being shared from one broken human to another.

So, to wrap this up...if you are expecting the coming pages to be religious quips and 'christianese' niceties...you may find "The Beautiful Ugly Truth" a disappointing read.

But if you can hang in there with her book and Study Guide, you will see how Gwen's pressing beyond her own fears and anxieties literally saved our marriage.

And I believe you will be inspired to press through to your own victory.

Mark Brague
Co-Founder
Reconnecting Lives Ministries

How to Use This Bible Study

The Beautiful Ugly Truth Study Guide is designed to be experienced in a small group setting. There is something cathartic about being together and encouraging one another in this journey. James even mentions how healing comes when we talk about the ways we have missed the mark and pray for one another (James 5:16 paraphrased). Can you do this study individually? Absolutely, but it is best experienced in a group. A facilitator is recommended to keep the discussion moving forward and have an awareness of time.

Materials Needed

In addition to bringing your Bible to the group discussions, each participant needs their individual study guide. We recommend each participant have a copy of *The Beautiful Ugly Truth*, but it is not required. The book is another investment of your time, and I believe it will bring encouragement to you on a journey that has been painful.

Format

- Attend the meetings, read over the weekly study, answer the questions, and process together.
- Between the sessions, complete the personal study guide portion for the following week.
- Read the suggested chapters in *The Beautiful Ugly Truth* at the end of each week and answer the personal questions. (Note that this is not required in order to participate in group discussion).

Timing of the Group

Each group meeting is timed for a two-hour session. Adhering to the suggested time will enable you to complete each session. You are encouraged to start with worship, move into a small prayer time, and then answer the questions during the weekly study along the way. Be sure to end with prayer. Lastly, trust in God that He will show up and heal hearts (Isaiah 61:1 AMP).

Facilitator

Each group should have a facilitator. This will enable the study to move along with questions asked in each week's study and for the timing of the meeting to be monitored. A facilitator will open in prayer, have others read, and have group questions to discuss giving each member the opportunity to discuss.

Personal Study

There will be suggested reading and some personal study questions to answer during the week. These questions will help strengthen the effect of the study before returning for the following week.

Closing Prayer

Close your time with prayer. Cover your participants in prayer for the week as they have opened up and shared vulnerable places in their lives. Allow them to share prayer requests. Remind them each week that God is leading them to a place of freedom.

Introduction

Responsibility

The Beautiful Ugly Truth STUDY GUIDE

This is a resource for rebuilding trust in God first and in other relationships after betrayal. Each week this study will guide you through some of the Kings in the Bible. You will read and answer questions throughout this study and then take your own personal study time questions home for the week. One week builds on the other until you have spelled the word; REBUILD.

I know if you have picked this study guide up, chances are you are either going through a betrayal or have been through one and are hurt by its destruction. Maybe your marriage is in shambles, or you feel betrayed by a family member or friend. Maybe you don't trust anyone anymore. And maybe you are questioning if God is even there for you. I just want you to know, God is for you. You are enough. You can do this. You are beautiful. And even though your current truth may be ugly, God specializes in making all things beautiful in its time.

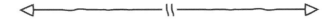

"He has made everything *beautiful* in its time."
Ecclesiastes 3:11a (ESV)

Betrayal is one of the most hurtful feelings we will experience in life. Typically, it announces its presence unexpectedly like a tornado and is felt throughout our whole being, only leaving in its path destruction. Sadness, anger, loneliness, and the entire grief wave pull at every part of your heart like nothing else. Because betrayal is so unexpected, the pain also yanks at our self-worth, leaving us full of questions and lots of doubts. Even though betrayal is inevitable, what we do with it makes all the difference in our lives.

At some level, we have all experienced some type of betrayal. It can be a marital betrayal, it can come from a family betrayal, a friend, a job, or even a church. Whatever your betrayal may be, I want to encourage you not to give in to the temptation to close your heart off. Instinctively, I know we want to close off our heart and hibernate. But we need to keep our hearts open so love can pour back into us. This doesn't mean you open yourself up to your betrayer, that will take time. But it does mean we need to keep our hearts open to those we trust and have our best interest at heart. Sadly, we don't get to pick and choose which emotions we want; we are created with all of them on purpose. So if we decide to build a fortress and cut off anger, disappointment, and hatred, we eventually cut off all of our other emotions including joy, peace, gratefulness, and love.

So the first step in healing from betrayal is to feel it. I know it is painful, and it seems counterproductive, but it is necessary. Allow yourself the time to travel along this journey, to feel every stage of grief. And remember, grief is not linear. One day you may feel anger, and one day you may feel sadness. And just when you think you are making progress in the sadness, you are ready to spit nails again. This is a normal part of the process. I remember being so afraid I would "get stuck" in one of the stages of grief, but it's quite the opposite. The sooner you allow yourself to feel and process the emotions and pain, the sooner healing will come. You can do this. You are becoming brave and becoming strong again. God is actually healing you through the process.

Since the release of *The Beautiful Ugly Truth* and Reconnecting Lives Ministries, we are frequently asked, "How do you rebuild trust?"

Trust is a valuable thing. Without it, relationships fall apart. Often my husband and I tell couples we coach that **forgiveness and trust are two different things**. We must forgive for our physical health and mental well-being, but **trust is earned**. Forgiveness is a gift we give ourselves and is between you and God. **Rebuilding trust takes believable behavior over a**

period of time. To sustain and rebuild a healthy relationship, we have to have both forgiveness and trust. So in my personal situation, not only did I need to find the strength to forgive Mark, my husband, but he also had to do the work of rebuilding trust to move forward in our relationship. Hidden secrets had to come to the surface in order for our relationship to be strong again. We each had to take responsibility for our actions. The first thing I realized was that I had deep-rooted trust issues. We all do, actually. I learned I had to reevaluate where I placed my trust.

Scripture is clear where NOT to place your trust.

Weapons . . . . Psalms 44:6
Wealth . . . . Psalms 49:6-7
Leaders . . . . Psalms 146:3
Humankind . . . . Jeremiah 17:5
Works . . . . Jeremiah 48:7
One's Righteousness . . Ezekiel 33:13

Scripture is clear where to put our trust.

God's Name . . . . Psalms 33:21
God's Word . . . . Psalms 119:42
In The Lord . . . . Jeremiah 17:7-8
Christ . . . . Matthew 12:17-21
God's Love . . . . I John 4:16

By definition the word Trust means… *a firm belief in the reliability, truth, ability, or strength of someone or something.*

I quickly understood the trust I placed in Mark was broken and I needed another source. I needed to rebuild my trust, not in Mark, but in something or someone who was unshakeable. Mark was human and broken with flaws. By definition, so was I. So are we all. Fortunately, I had been taught my whole life that God was faithful and trustworthy. I can lean completely on Him and His Word. Rebuilding trust for me had to start with rebuilding trust in God during this process.

Once the blinders were open in Mark's eyes, he began to take the first step in rebuilding trust with me. He recognized the damage caused and began to take responsibility for his actions.

If you want to rebuild trust in God or any other relationship, here are a few steps you will need to take. Each step will correlate with each week of the study. It's designed that way to help you process each step.

We will use the acronym for REBUILD.

The R in this Introduction section will be one of the most valuable steps. R stands for Responsibility—you must take it. If you want to rebuild trust, you have to recognize the damage that has been done and begin to take responsibility. The work you will do to take responsibility will depend on whether you are the betrayed or the betrayer. If you have been betrayed, your step of responsibility is rebuilding trust in God and allowing yourself to grieve. If you have been the betrayer, taking responsibility for your actions will aid in rebuilding trust in others.

Responsibility.   Introduction

This is the valley of rebuilding broken-down places. You are already engaging in the process IF you are doing this study. And if we want to rebuild trust with God and others, we must take this critical first step. We need to take responsibility. Responsibility for the process. Responsibility takes actions. It's sometimes difficult to look in a mirror and own our actions, but if we want to build trust with others we must start with ourselves. Trust can be rebuilt but this stage will take some time. Not only do you need to demonstrate you have learned from your mistakes, you have to show others you understand and that you have changed.

Empathy.   Week 1: The Valley of Decision and Betrayal

It's the ability to walk a mile in another's skin. No one walked a mile in our shoes more than our Savior. And Jesus, He knows about betrayal. He conquered it, and so will you. Finding empathy for someone who has hurt us is understandably difficult, but the power to forgive will release you from the pain. However, we cannot confuse forgiveness with trust or grief. We can decide to forgive but rebuilding trust will take time. Remember, trust is earned. But YOU will need to decide to forgive before the other steps work. Forgiveness is a gift for you, I promise.

Build.   Week 2: The Valley of the High Places

You are building something here. But most of the time before you build up, you have to tear down. We must look at the foundation. What needs to be demolished in order to build a firm foundation? What is our foundation built upon? Be open to self growth and improvement. Betrayal changes everyone. This is the place where we need to start fresh not only with others, but with God.

Unity.   Week 3: The Valley in our Own Mind; from Restoration to Reformation

Be aware of your innermost feelings and share your thoughts. Don't be afraid. God is leading you to a good place. You can trust Him through the battles. Unity is a building block for rebuilding trust. We might not be able to trust our betrayer, but as we learned, God wants unity with us. You can trust Him. And where there is unity, it is here God commands the blessing (Psalms 133).

Imagine.   Week 4: The Valley for our Identity and Legacy

Can you imagine this betrayal is leading you to a healthier place? If you have chosen to rebuild trust with God and others, ask for what you need from each other respectfully. You can no longer go along with the crowd and take offense. Be honest about your goals and check in with each other regularly. This stage is for you, your identity, but most importantly, how your identity will affect your legacy. Dream big. Imagine wholeness. God has good things in mind for you.

Listen.   Week 5: The Valley of Transformation

This is the battle of transformation. This is when God is calling you to face your giants. You are no longer a victim. Part of trusting is listening to what God says, how He instructs you, and what He calls you to do. What He calls you to may go against what your flesh and mind are telling you to do. But learning to trust in the valley will lead to a beautiful legacy.

Decide.   Week 6: The Valley Shall Be Raised Up

Here we meet King Jesus. If anyone had the power and the right to do something different, He did. Jesus even asked God if there was another way to bring restoration and resurrection to the process. Yet He humbled Himself and died in our place. No one was more aware of betrayal and how to overcome it than Jesus.

I believe this study will draw you closer to God and all your other relationships. It will provide joy, deliverance, safety, inheritance, and guidance on your journey. It is, indeed, *The Beautiful Ugly Truth*. Along our journey of rebuilding trust, we will study some kings of the Old Testament and the battles they faced. We will study the valleys they endured and the decisions they made, some good and some not so good. Most importantly, we will discover where God was in the process. When hard times come, we often question if God changed His mind or His plans for us. We begin to doubt ourselves and if we really heard God. Sometimes we even question why God allowed such betrayal to happen. God is with you, my friend. He has not forsaken you, and He will not fail you. We only give the enemy territory by putting walls over our hearts and closing people out. But when faith is restored and trust is rebuilt, we will see how God has always been for His people. These Old Testament kings will show us the way.

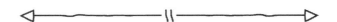

"Are you tired? Worn out? Burned out on religion? Come to me. Get away with me and you'll *recover* your life. I'll show you how to take a real *rest*. Walk with me and work with me—watch how I do it. Learn the unforced rhythms of *grace*. I won't lay anything heavy or ill-fitting on you. Keep company with me and you'll learn to live *freely* and *lightly*."

Matthew 11:28-30 (MSG)

Personal Study

Suggested Reading: Chapter 1 in *The Beautiful Ugly Truth*.

Ask God what you need to take responsibility for.

_____

_____

_____

_____

Is there a relationship in which you would like to rebuild trust?

_____

_____

_____

_____

What steps can you take to rebuild trust?

_____

_____

_____

_____

Week 1 – The Valley of Decision

Empathy

Today, we will begin our journey together for the next six weeks. If you missed the Introduction, please go back and read it. It is critical to the process of rebuilding trust. I am excited to introduce you to *The Beautiful Ugly Truth Bible Study*. I believe we all have an area or areas in which we desire God to heal. When we have been hurt and betrayed, I have learned that trusting someone can become a challenge. We actually, maybe even secretly, begin to distrust. We distrust our spouse, family member, friend, doctor, co-worker, and sometimes, yes, we even begin to distrust God. Our thought process can be full of questions. We are in a valley of decisions.

And if we distrust, and your mind is full of questions, I have another question for you: Do you need to forgive someone? Maybe you are ready to throw down this study and declare that no one would understand what you have endured. Yet forgiveness is key in the process of rebuilding trust. Maybe not in your betrayer at first, but with God and others. Forgiveness is not letting the offender off the hook; it's actually providing an escape for you. **Unforgiveness wants to build a bridge to our wound and allow us to pass back and forth on the bridge and drink from its pain.** I am not saying today or tomorrow, but in God's timing forgiveness will set you free from the pain of betrayal. Forgiveness keeps any bitterness from taking root when our heart is hurting.

My husband and I coach couples and tell them forgiveness and trust are two different things. Often these feelings are considered one in our own thinking. Forgiveness does not mean you trust someone. And mixed in between those two huge words is grief. Betrayal can be messy to our human mind. Yet, we need to walk through the grieving process in order to rebuild trust. Grief means you have lost something. And grieving the loss of something is also part of the healing process. It's so vital to our health: mental, physical, and spiritual. So in these next six weeks, we will study God's Word, pray together, and watch God do what He does best, heal us.

So let's really start. Who do you need to forgive? Write it out, and spell the name as if you were praying and giving this to God.

_____

_____

_____

_____

During our betrayal season, I saw this sign in a hospital gift shop:

"Someday, everything will make *perfect* sense."

I wasn't sure how God would make sense of this heartbreaking season in my marriage, but I knew He could. I also believe someday, everything you are walking through will make perfect sense, too. Yet every time we are wronged, we go through temptation, anger, and some sense of entitlement. I learned you will be led into more temptation when you choose not to forgive.

What is your definition of betrayal?

_____

_____

_____

_____

What type of betrayal have you experienced that you want God to heal? Please journal below as we begin.

_____

_____

_____

_____

Betrayal becomes an issue of trust only because our hearts are involved. Once you have been betrayed, it's not unusual to think about other times when trust was compromised. Unhealed wounds beget unhealed wounds, and our response to them can cause a downward spiral in our physical life, emotional thought process, and spiritual well-being. **When we have been betrayed, we need to respond differently to break the downward spiral cycle in our thoughts and feelings.** I call this process flesh burning. I know what God is calling me to do, but my flesh wants to have its own way. If the betrayal has been most recent, grieving and all the feelings; denial, anger, bargaining, depression, and acceptance, associated with grief are healthy. These feelings are helping us process our new reality. But if betrayal happened years ago, this is what I mean by "responding differently" in order to walk in health.

My prayer through this study is that you will see betrayal as a gift in disguise. Sadly, we live in a broken world. I am not in any way saying Jesus caused the betrayal. But I am saying Jesus can certainly use it. I also understand betrayal doesn't feel much like a gift during the moment, actually quite the opposite. I am so sorry for your pain, friend. But God can use what the enemy meant to destroy you with and take it to re-establish our trust in Him and others. **I believe the enemy's purpose for betrayal is to break our trust with Father God.** If we don't trust God, we lose territory in life and our calling.

Thankfully Jesus, our Savior, knew something about betrayal. Jesus was betrayed. And He defeated betrayal, and brought restoration and resurrection to it. And He taught us how to trust in Him again. So let's hang out this week with the most amazing King.

Read Hebrews 13:8. What do we know about Jesus?

_____

_____

_____

_____

Read Hebrews 4:15-16. What are the two things we can gain when we draw near to the throne of grace in verse 16?

_____

_____

_____

_____

Jesus is the same yesterday, today, and forever. He is our High Priest, acquainted with our weakness. He faced what we have faced, yet without sin. What a better teacher to learn from? As we draw near to Him with confidence, He will give us mercy and grace.

Several years ago, I had the honor to go to Israel. I walked where our Savior walked, healed, lived, died, resurrected, and now we are awaiting His return. Until then, I decided I want to live as Jesus lived, and love like Jesus loved. He knows a few things about betrayal, and even though this is not an easy journey, we can trust Him. Let's go to Him with our betrayal.

Let's read John 18:1-18, Matthew 26:47-56, Mark 14:43-52, or Luke 22:47-53. What stands out to you in these verses?

_____

_____

_____

_____

Each of the four gospels tells this story. Jesus was getting ready to be betrayed by Judas, arrested, and crucified. Jesus had just prayed to the Father in John 17 and refers to that in John 18:1.

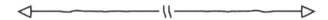

"When Jesus had spoken these words, he went out with his disciples across the brook *Kidron,* where there was a *garden,* which he and his disciples entered."

John 18:1 (ESV)

What is the Kidron Valley or the Brook Kidron? And why did Jesus have to go across it to get to the garden? It begged the question, is the Brook Kidron something we have to go across?

The Kidron Valley in Israel

The Brook Kidron is East of Jerusalem, leading to the Mountain of Olives. This valley actually means "The Valley of Decision." And this valley is also known as the "Shadow of Death." Jesus actually walked across the Kidron Valley after his betrayal, on His way to the Garden of Gethsemane. I believe the Brook (or valley) Kidron teaches us something very valuable about betrayal and overcoming it.

Where else in scripture is the *Shadow of Death* mentioned?

_____

_____

_____

_____

Read Psalm 23:4. Write the verse here.

_____

_____

_____

_____

What will I fear in this verse?

_____

_____

_____

_____

Who is with us when we walk through our *Shadow of Death*?

_____

_____

_____

_____

In Hebrew, the name Kidron means gloomy, ashy, dark, black color like sackcloth. It is known as a place of mourning, sorrow, and even death. This actual place was given to idol worship and became a major cemetery reference many times in the Old Testament. Yet Jesus walked through this valley Kidron and conquered this place.

The first mention of the Kidron Valley was in 2 Samuel 15:23 when David flees through the Brook Kidron, also *AFTER* a betrayal of Absalom, his son, to the Mount of Olives. Betrayal certainly takes us to a gloomy, ashy, dark place of mourning. We wonder if we will see the light of day again. We will. One day. Yet it is here, I believe, that the Brook Kidron becomes our very own personal "Valley of Decision."

I love how scripture says Jesus went with His disciples across the Brook Kidron where there was a garden. **The Brook Kidron is one of the most important crucibles we will face in our lives on the way to our restoration and resurrection.** When we follow Jesus through our betrayal, He will lead us through the valley, to our garden, and then to our victory.

However, before the resurrection of something, I discovered several things about betrayal.

1. There is always a cost to betrayal. (Matthew 26:15)

2. There is always a trap or a plot to betrayal. (Matthew 26:16)
3. Jesus will provide freedom from betrayal. (Matthew 26:26-28)

Typically, betrayal hurts so deeply because it is with someone we trusted. We often ask two questions:

1. How do I heal?
2. How do I trust again?

In this study, we will heal and learn how to rebuild trust again. Jesus will walk beside us along the way and make every crooked place in our path straight again. We must know, above all, Jesus is trustworthy. When we need our trust restored, we must go to the Restorer.

Read Matthew 6:14-15. What does God say about forgiving others? What happens if I do not forgive others?

_____

_____

_____

_____

I learned that forgiveness was my responsibility. I could choose not to forgive, but what would be my gain?

It was clear that in order for me to understand the gift in all the madness, I must have empathy and learn to forgive.

Empathy is the ability to understand and share the feelings of another. Understanding the brokenness in others helps us process our feelings. Christ modeled empathy for you as He walked over the Brook Kidron. He made the decision to pursue God's will. He knew He would be betrayed, yet He made the decision to forgive in His valley to demonstrate His love for us and even those who would betray Him. Empathy is also part of the rebuilding process.

I completely understand, and know of the battle raging in your own mind. I was there. It was difficult to forgive my betrayer but it was necessary for healing. Part of rebuilding trust is a willingness to walk in forgiveness.

Spend some time and ask God who you need help forgiving. Write a prayer below.

_____

_____

_____

_____

I will be honest, I did not feel like forgiving when my heart was so broken. The lines above might still be blank and it's okay for now. My prayer for you is that by the end of this study the lines above will be filled in.

I thought forgiving would mean I was letting my betrayer off the hook. But I quickly learned that forgiving was letting me off the hook. It was my first step to restoration.

Lysa Terkheurst once said, "*Hurt feelings sometimes don't coincide with holy instructions.*"

Your feelings are probably the last thing that you want to come alongside you on this journey. However, I decided I did not want anyone to high-jack my walk with Christ, especially my betrayer. Proverbs 19:16 (TPT) says, "Honor God's holy instructions and life will go well for you."

Betrayal causes damage. And when we step back and see it from an aerial view, we will also witness the collateral damage. This was when I discovered there were layers to forgiveness. **Not only do we need to forgive the one who hurt us but forgive the impact of the hurt caused.** Just because you forgave and still feel anger does not mean you are a failure at this whole forgiveness thing. It just means there was a deep impact. We will be triggered along the way. **It does not mean you have not forgiven the person, it just means there are layers our Savior wants to lead you through.** Forgiving the impact when we are triggered is just building new highways in our brain to healthier living. Triggers are a sign your brain desires a different path.

I believe God is leading you onto a deeper path with more intimacy. Past all the things we can see in the natural and into a path of abiding peace. He is leading us to a place of rebuilding trust in Him and a place of abundance. Remember Jesus walked across the Kidron Valley with His disciples, and HE is with you today as you walk across your personal Brook Kidron. What may feel like death today through the valley and to a garden, will feel different as we travel along. And I promise… He has resurrection in mind for you. Jesus is our true Resurrected King who battled everything and every enemy we face today. He laid everything we would face to rest and now calls us to rise with Him.

Close in prayer.

_____

_____

_____

_____

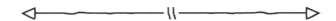

"Arise, shine, for your light has come, and the *glory* of the LORD has risen upon you."

Isaiah 60:1 (ESV)

Personal Study

Suggested Reading: Chapters 2-3 in *The Beautiful Ugly Truth*.

We all have experienced emotional trauma in our lives growing up. Are you aware of any wounds you received growing up that God wants to heal?

_____

_____

_____

_____

Who do you need to forgive to move forward?

_____

_____

_____

_____

What is God telling you about your personal Brook Kidron?

_____

_____

_____

_____

Write below or on index cards how you have been hurt. Look at each card and pray, "I am choosing to forgive." Don't look for warm fuzzies. Just choose to forgive.

Week 2 – The Valley of High Places

Build

Today, we are going to build. But before we build anything, we must lay a foundation. And before we build a new foundation, we must tear down and clear a new path. You can trust God. He is making all things new, even with you.

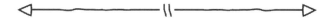

"Remember not the former things, nor consider the things of old. Behold, I am doing a *new* thing; now it springs forth, do you not perceive it? I will make a way in the wilderness and rivers in the desert."

Isaiah 43:18-19 (ESV)

"I wanted to trust God, but I didn't…"

And sadly, my broken marriage was a reminder of that statement to me. How do you rebuild on betrayal? Remember when I wrote *unhealed wounds beget unhealed wounds*? Maybe the secret to my healing was in the first sentence of this week's study. "I wanted to trust God, but I didn't." Maybe said another way was that I didn't trust God with my whole heart. Don't get me wrong, I had said the sinner's prayer and had served God in ministry for years, but trusting God with my whole heart? I would have told anyone and everyone I trusted God, but my brokenness was telling a different story. Maybe Father God was taking me deeper into our relationship. Perhaps there is some truth there for you, too. I had walked through lots of healing at this point in my life, but if something triggered me, or God's timing took longer than expected, or his lack of intervention seemed slow, I doubted His provision for me. It didn't take long for me to develop trust issues in my life. So keeping part of my whole heart for safe keeping seemed normal to me.

Most of the time, trust issues begin when we are very young, as mine did. I had measures of healing along my broken path, but when the one I thought would never hurt me or betray me did, it magnified my distrust in humankind and God. I remember when my counselor told me, "*Until you can trust Mark, trust God in Mark.*" Boy, I had to figure some things out. Don't get me wrong, I was a Jesus girl to my bones but feeling out of control in my marriage and my life led me on a hunt for solutions on my own. I wanted answers, and if God didn't move fast enough for my liking, I was more than happy to go to the altar of my own fixing. I will do it my way. I've got this. And secretly, nobody is going to tell me what to do. Sadly, not all well-intended solutions honor God.

Let me say, God has been faithful. He has healed my trust issues. At least the ones I know about. He has healed my marriage, and He has healed my perception of Him. It's amazing how **God often gets the blame for misfortune in our lives.** Trusting and healing take time. And for me, it required a much closer relationship with God to figure out the finer details. I had to open up my heart and walk the path of an intimate relationship with Him. Just me, God, and His Word. I discovered the more you know God, the more you will trust Him. And in that knowledge, WE are becoming. Becoming what? Mature believers in the faith. The moment I confessed my sins, I became, but I wasn't quite mature. His Spirit taught me I am always becoming.

The Apostle Paul spoke of this when he wrote the letter to the Galatians. The moment we accept Christ as our redeemer, we are heirs. But we are not perfect. We are minors growing up in the Father's house.

"As long as an heir is a minor, he's not really much different than a servant, although he's master over all of them. For until the time appointed by the father, the child is under the domestic supervision of the guardians of the estate."

Galatians 4:1-2 (TPT)

So, the searing issue during the upheaval of my marriage was my trust issues. The biggest of all my issues…distrust, a spiritual erosion of sorts. I can feel anxious, exhausted, and fearful, but without trust, all the unwanted feelings follow along, making way for an erosion of myself and my relationship with God the Father. If God loved me, why would He let this happen? It was because God loved me that He allowed it. He knows the treasures we will find when we seek after Him. He uses trials so we can grow into an heir.

Just like Mark had to go to the root of his issues, I had to go to the root of mine and start digging. I had to learn how to rebuild trust again, not only with Mark, but with God. If the enemy of our soul can keep us from trusting in God, he knows we will turn away from God. It's an offense. God does not want that for you. It's been years since the experience, but as I seek our faithful Father, He reveals more and more of Himself to me, along with His character. He is a good God.

Maybe marital issues are not where you land on the spectrum of betrayal, rejection, or distrust. Betrayal comes from any broken relationship. And betrayal leads to brokenness in trust. And broken trust leads to distrust in every other area in our lives. Wherever there are areas of distrust, God wants to heal and bring you closer to Him. He has a destiny in mind for you.

As I studied how to rebuild trust, God began to reveal my heart. He showed me all the places I had set up fake altars in my own life. I call them "high places" or lack of trust. Distrust, quite honestly. So what were "high places" in the Bible, and how did they reveal distrust? Let's see what God's Word calls high places.

Today, we will study King Solomon. He was one of the sons of King David. To set up where we are in the story, King Saul's kingdom was stripped from him, and David was anointed King. David fought, and won many, many battles but made some poor decisions along the way. Several of which we have probably all read about. We will study King David later. But first, we will look at the life of King Solomon and what high places are.

We first read about high places in the Old Testament. It was a place of worship dedicated to OTHER gods. At these high places, God's people would make sacrifices, burn incense, and hold feasts or festivals.

Read 1 Kings 3:1-2. Why would the people sacrifice at the high places?

_____

_____

_____

_____

Because no house had yet been built for the name of the Lord, high places were places of worship on elevated pieces of land. My first-hand experience with seeing a high place was in 2019 when I traveled to Israel with a group of friends.

The Altar of Dan

The high place in Dan was a ritual site established by King Jeroboam, son of Nebet, as an "alternative" worship site for Jerusalem. At the high places, you worshiped your god of choosing. The Holy Temple Solomon would build had not been constructed yet. The Bible describes Jeroboam erecting a golden calf and building an altar at Dan (1 Kings 12:28-31). Does a golden calf and a false altar sound familiar? The King would take counsel here of his own liking and would say to the Israelites, "You have gone up to Jerusalem long enough." There was a high place for worship erected in Bethal and this one in Dan, just in case Jerusalem was too far to travel.

But as we review, when the Israelites first entered the promised land, they were told to destroy ALL the high places, idols, and images.

Read Numbers 33:50-53. What was God's instruction to the people as they entered the promised land?

_____

_____

_____

_____

Please note here, it is AFTER God's people enter into their promised land that God instructs the demolishing of other high places. Idol worship. I believe when we trust God and turn to Him, we have walked into our promised land. It is here God just might expose some high places in our own lives. His desire is for you to only worship Him. But we will see that sometimes our greatest test comes after our greatest victory.

High places were considered "acceptable" until King Solomon finished the temple. Priests would accept offerings at these high places. The temple, built in Jerusalem by Solomon, was to usher in a new period of worship for the Israelites. But despite this new temple, God's people were still found worshiping at other high places to gods of their culture. The high places became idol worship after God instructed for them to be torn down. These high places included gods of fertility, thunder and rain gods, golden calves, gods that included sacrifices of animals and children, and Asherah poles.

Often, I read *over* these high places and Asherah poles in scripture as they were more historical to me. I get it…don't worship idols. Idols are bad. But there was a reason God would instruct each King of Israel to remove all of the high places and Asherah poles. As we have learned, high places were places of idol worship.

What were Asherah poles? As I began to study Asherah poles, I discovered Asherah was one of the goddesses of the Canaanites. The symbol was of females that were naked, sometimes pregnant, with exaggerated breasts that she held out promising her followers fertility. The Bible indicates she was worshiped near trees and poles, hence their names. These were alarming to me. They were tied to sexual immorality, darkness, seductive practices, and ritual sex. Maybe we would call it pornography in our day and time. Asherah was believed to be Baal's mother, and she was also his mistress. The Canaanites attributed their fertility to this god. It's amazing how the enemy twists pornography as a way to "spice up your sex life," much like Asherah poles in biblical days. The book of Judges reveals the ongoing struggle the Israelites' had with Canaanite worship and culture. Throughout the Old Testament, anytime God instructed his people to tear down the high places, Asherah poles were always mentioned.

Often a new king would step into His reign (His promised land) and be asked by the prophets of God to destroy the high places and the Asherah poles. Let's look at King Solomon.

What did King Solomon ask God for in 1 Kings 3:1-15? Specifically, in verse 9.

_____

_____

_____

_____

Full of understanding of God and wisdom to rule, King Solomon was known for trusting God and honoring His ways. With that came promises from God that he would be the King of Israel, known for building the Holy Temple of God and establishing his royal throne over Israel forever.

What did God promise King Solomon in 1 Kings 9:3-5 after King Solomon finished the Holy Temple?

_____

_____

_____

_____

Read 1 Kings 9:6-9. If King Solomon turned aside from following God and did not keep His commandments and statutes by worshiping other gods, what would happen to the house Solomon built for God in verse 8?

_____

_____

_____

_____

Even though Solomon was full of wisdom, he had a shortcoming. Maybe an area he didn't completely trust God with. Let's read about it in 1 Kings 11:1.

What did Solomon love more, or what would you say was King Solomon's shortcoming?

_____

_____

_____

_____

Read 1 Kings 11:1-8. His wives turned his heart after other gods, and his heart was not wholly true to the Lord his God. Women have the power of influence, and because of this, Solomon's wives caused him to worship many gods, their gods. Solomon's decision to not only worship the Lord but all the other gods was part of his destruction. The Lord told Solomon He would tear his kingdom away from him if he continued to worship at these other altars. When King Solomon constructed the Holy Temple in Israel to the Lord for offerings and worship, high places were no longer acceptable. The temple King Solomon built was a sign of a new era, a new season. However, the foreign wives of King Solomon became more and more acceptable to the king, and because of it, the temple lies in ruins today.

The Ruins of Solomon's Temple in Jerusalem

Likewise, God will usher us into a new season, and when we turn and worship the decisions of our past, our promises can lay in ruins also. I made altars of my own decisions, but God was telling me **my broken, dark season was actually the beginning of something new in my life**.

So how does all of this relate to trust? Or to me? Or to you?

While we don't have physical "high places" today…we do have issues. Many times our issues cause us to take matters into our own hands. And culture can pressure us to go along with the norm. Rarely does the cultural norm line up with God's will or processes. Maybe we don't call our issues "high places" today, but "high places" are where people elevate other things over God's will and processes. When we take matters into our own hands, for whatever reason, we are worshiping our own way of doing things rather than trusting God's promises and provision for our lives.

Today, I believe the ways in which we mishandle our trust issues would be called high places of idolatry. And if it was an issue for the kings in the Old Testament, I knew I needed to do more investigating. If God instructed mighty kings to destroy high places, to trust Him more, and obey Him wholeheartedly, maybe we need to consider if there are obstacles in our hearts that prevent us from trusting God fully and entering into our new promised land.

High places are where we elevate our abilities and lower our faith in God. Places where we trust in our own abilities more than trusting what God told us to do.

We may not refer to our trust issues as 'high places of worship,' and we may not have Asherah poles like King Solomon did, but what do you think modern-day idols would be for us?

_____

_____

_____

_____

I am not sure what steps of obedience God is calling you to in order to claim your promises from Him, but you can trust Him. Trusting God and walking in His ways rather than our own abilities allows us to take more kingdom territory. We must be willing to step outside our comfort zone and trust His plan. His plan is still good and can be trusted.

As I studied the notable kings, the battles they fought, and the valleys they met in, it is interesting to know that King Solomon never fought in any battles. His father, David, had fought many battles and subdued enemies surrounding Israel. Yet, his son did not.

King Solomon's name actually means *peace*. It comes from the root Hebrew word that means *to replace or to restore*. Like Solomon, some of the battles you are enduring or endured will only mean a place of peace for your children. Or perhaps the battles your parents achieved victory over means you will walk in peace.

His monumental accomplishment was the construction of the Temple of God and restoring God's place of worship for Israel rather than the idols of high places. It seemed unusual that he had peace throughout his reign because he made many alliances with various other kingdoms by marrying their king's daughters when God told him not to.

Trusting God is one of the most important things we can do. The enemy of our soul comes to try to get us to distrust God and erect high places of worship in our own lives to keep us from entering into all our promises. Honestly, we may not understand why we are walking the path God has us on currently, but He is worthy and can be trusted. As we lean into Him and ask Him to reveal and heal areas of distrust, we will soon see that we are putting one step in front of the other and walking into our dream, our purpose, and our destiny. Remember, the soil around our seed is vital, but the seed in us during our darkest season has all the power it needs to become and flourish. We have entered our promised land, friend. Do not misunderstand the place of planting for a burial. It may feel like a dark, dry place but God is preparing you to bear fruit.

What is God showing you now or speaking to you here? Please write below if you feel like you have places where you have not trusted God.

_____

_____

_____

_____

In Chapter 3 of *The Beautiful Ugly Truth*, I talk about our four basic needs that come from God (pg 76).

If our basic needs of, affirmation, security, purpose, and identity do not come from God, we are likely to have areas of distrust and worship the making of our own solutions. As mentioned in Chapter 3, the woman at the well in John 4:4-42 is where Jesus met a very thirsty woman. Is it any surprise Samaria was where King Ahab built a temple to Baal, another false God? It is here we must search our real life Samaria (some-area) and discover our thirst and let Jesus quench it to take us further into our promised land.

Which of the four basic needs do you need most from God in this season of your life?

_____

_____

_____

_____

When we are willing to obey God and understand that He is a good God who only asks things of us for our best, we will grow to completely trust Him more and more. Distrust is a "High Place" of worship, and once we repent, turn and trust God, we can rebuild trust in others.

Don't fear the journey… God has healing in mind. We all have experienced emotional trauma in our lives growing up. Do you know of any wounds or emotional trauma God wants to heal?

_____

_____

_____

_____

Where do you feel like you have created a "high place" to worship other than God? For example: distrust, inner vows that no one would ever hurt you again, unforgiveness, rejection of others, anger towards God.

_____

_____

_____

_____

Close in prayer.

_____

_____

_____

_____

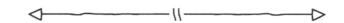

"Fear not for I am with you; be not dismayed, for I am your God; I will *strengthen* you, I will *help* you, I will *uphold* you with my righteous right hand."

Isaiah 41:10 (ESV)

Personal Study

Suggested Reading: Chapter 4 in *The Beautiful Ugly Truth*.

What do you believe your high places are?

_____

_____

_____

_____

Now that we have recognized where we have built high places of distrust, what do you want to rebuild with God?

_____

_____

_____

_____

God has given you a safe place to land, who do you need to give a safe place to land?

_____

_____

_____

_____

Week 3 – The Valley in Our Own Mind

Unity

More than anything, God desires unity. King David even wrote about unity in the Psalms. He said, "Behold, how good and pleasant it is when brothers dwell in unity!" (Psalm 133:1 ESV).

In Psalms 133:3 (ESV), what did David say the Lord commanded when there was unity?

_____

_____

_____

_____

Today, we will study the great King Hezekiah.

The death of something is really the birthing of something else. This was something I learned during our betrayal season. The question I had to ask myself, and you will have to ask yourself is, "Do I trust God enough to walk through the death of something to experience the birth of something else?"

This is typically a very *crucial* place in our lives and our hearts. More questions than answers arise during this time. We ponder questions like: Will I trust again? Who can I trust? Do I trust God? What was wrong with the way things were? Will I embrace the process of restoration and reformation? Will I walk through the dying process in life to experience something new?

The definition of the word *crucial* goes further in explaining what a crossroads we are at.

Crucial by definition is, *decisive or critical, especially in the success or failure of something. It's of great importance.*

I mention in chapter five of my book that I am an Interior Designer by trade. I have worked with restoration companies and seen all kinds of scopes of work. I've seen and even experienced my own kitchen and bathroom remodels. But I have also witnessed walking into a room that shows the bare studs, electrical wires, and plumbing pipes exposed. No way to turn on a light or turn on the water through a sink. I have seen my share of fire damage and water damage and the destruction it laid. And once or twice I have seen a complete rebuild. It's a stressful time when things in life do not feel put together. I have experienced this physically and emotionally. Where my heart lay bare, and any connection with my spouse and God felt exposed and unprotected.

No matter what is required to restore a room, a house, or our hearts, the most important part of this process is to never stop in the middle. Imagine walking into a half-finished remodel and throwing a hammer down, and telling your general contractor he is fired because you cannot handle the time it is taking anymore. You are tired of the delays and the expanding budget. You are over the disappointment of costly repairs and just when you thought you are moving forward and making progress, you experience another setback. It's a crucial time. Do you trust the process OR do you stop?

Even as a designer, I am not capable of finishing this type of work on my own. I can get a vision of what needs to be done, but I cannot complete the work without a general contractor or a carpenter. Our life in our promised land will have giants that need to be slain. Giants come with the land. But once we realize we are here…we must build an altar, worship God for who He is, and then partner with Him to go to work. We need unity with God before we can rebuild unity with others. Unity is a building block to restore trust. We have to destroy all the high places we have turned to and worshiped and trust God for the completion. Remember, high places in the Old Testament were places people worshiped gods other than the one true God of Israel. Our high places can even be the things we believe about God that are just not true. Our high places can also be our way of showing ourselves comfort emotionally when we don't trust others. Picture Jesus as your contractor, and let your trust grow in Him. I promise, He will finish what He starts.

Please read Philippians 1:6. What are you believing God to accomplish for you confidently?

_____

_____

_____

_____

Do you trust God will finish what He started? What steps do you need to take?

_____

_____

_____

_____

We are halfway through the study; we either worship the gods of culture, embrace all of our unfinished work and build inner walls in our hearts to protect our pain, or we can decide to partner with God, the process, and wait confidently for the revealing of what God will complete in us. This crucial place is when we see ourselves in a mirror. God is showing us areas we need to change. Is there responsibility we need to take to get healthy? Is there empathy we need to show ourselves or others? Are there altars of doing things our own way that we need to destroy?

We are on our way to unity. And God commands the blessing where He sees unity. Here is where we meet King Hezekiah, King of the Southern Kingdom. Israel has been divided into the Northern Kingdom and the Southern Kingdom. King Solomon and his reign of peace have come to an end. The people of God began living through some very rough, difficult times. Many godly and ungodly kings were at the helm of these kingdoms before Hezekiah. Division in the kings and the kingdoms laid waste most of Israel. Wars, idol worship, and high places were the norm, and people's hearts turned to fear. Slavery was more than a racial issue. It was unknown when the next wave of evil would rear its ugly head. Along with sickness and disease, Israel felt exposed. The Northern Kingdom had fallen captive to the Assyrian army, and God's people, if not in captivity, had run into exile to try to hide. Some fled to find shelter in the Southern Kingdom and found King Hezekiah on the throne. 2 Kings 18 and 2 Chronicles 32 tell the story of the great King Hezekiah.

Read 2 Kings 18:1-4 and write down what you learned about King Hezekiah. What did he do?

_____

_____

_____

_____

In verse 5 of the same chapter, we learned King Hezekiah *trusted in the Lord, the God of Israel, so that there was none like him among all of the kings of Judah after him, nor among those who were before him, (2 Kings 18:5 ESV).*

Finally, scripture said the Lord was with Hezekiah wherever he went, and he prospered in all he did. In King Hezekiah's 4th year of reign over the Southern Kingdom, the Northern Kingdom of Samaria fell. The king of Assyria, Shalmaneser, came against Israel's Northern Kingdom and captured it. There were many battles while Hezekiah reigned for twenty-nine years. Most notable was against the Assyrian army, who also wanted to capture the Southern Kingdom of Judah. At one point, in a weak moment, Hezekiah paid off the king of the Assyrian army, Sennacherib (suh.na.kr.ib), to just go away. Yet a pay off or bribe is never good and typically dishonest, at best. Hezekiah repents to God, comes back in unity with God, and fortifies the city of Jerusalem.

While we were in Israel in 2019, we learned water and its supply was the most important thing when kings went into battle. Most armies would capture a city by finding and cutting off the cities' water supply. If the attacking army could find the source of water and cut it off, victory was certain. Knowing this, King Hezekiah built a tunnel 1,750 feet long through Jerusalem. This tunnel was cut through the rock beneath the City of David, leading water through Gihon to the Siloam Pool, which was a reservoir of fresh water at the end of the tunnel.

Hezekiah's Tunnel

Why is water so important in scripture and in our life?

_____

_____

_____

_____

Because your enemy knows your source of water, he is no different from times of old. He wants territory in your life, so he will come to attack your water supply. What does scripture call living water? Read Jeremiah 2:13, Jeremiah 17:13, and John 4:10.

_____

_____

_____

_____

After we do the work of tearing down our high places, the enemy comes, mocks our fortified cities, and tries to find your water source next, which is our unity with God. He knows if he can cut off your water supply, our "Living Water," like in the Old Testament, then his victory is certain. During our most difficult season of betrayal, it's very important to stay close to God's Word. That is why our beloved Christ told the woman at the well in John 4,

"…but whoever drinks of the water that I will
give him will never be thirsty again."

John 4:14 (ESV)

Even though King Hezekiah had paid off Sennacherib earlier in his reign, the Assyrian army returned to attack the Southern Kingdom again. But this time was different.

In 2 Kings 18:19-23, what was one of the questions Rabshakeh asked King Hezekiah that stands out to you?

_____

_____

_____

_____

Rabshakeh was the "Chief of the Princes." He was the field commander sent by Sennacherib, the king of the Assyrian army. "Say to Hezehiah, 'Thus says the great king, the king of Assyria: On what do you rest this trust of yours?'" (2 Kings 18:19).

And in the same chapter, in verse 22, what did Rabshakeh remind the people of Israel that their King Hezekiah had done? And in verse 23, what did Rabshakeh want the people of God to do? (2 Kings 18: 22-23).

_____

_____

_____

_____

When we decide we will walk in freedom and rebuild trust in the Lord and His commands wholeheartedly, the enemy lays down some trash talk and comes to mock us and offers us a wager to turn our loyalty back to the dark side. Fear mocks us in our promised land when we turn our affections towards the Lord to rebuild trust in Him and Him only. And fear must be removed.

As I studied these chapters, it was interesting to discover the meaning of names. Names are so important. The King of the Assyrian army, Sennacherib, in Hebrew, means *sin* and *has replaced my brothers*. Isn't it like sin to come take us captive and mock us for rebuilding trust in the Lord?

Sometimes our battles, like Hezekiah, come to our own back door. We didn't ask for it. It just showed up. The Assyrian King wanted to take Hezekiah and the people of Jerusalem captive. And "sin" wants to take us captive. Our response to rebuilding trust in the Lord will determine our outcome.

The king continues to mock God's people and Hezekiah. What does the King of Assyria say to the people in 2 Kings 18:31-32?

_____

_____

_____

_____

Make peace with sin? "Sin," like Sennacherib, offers us a counterfeit to our promised land. Hezekiah's most notable battle was in his own land of Jerusalem. Jerusalem in Hebrew means, *City of Peace.* Sometimes our valley experience, like Hezekiah's, is in protecting our peace which is in us and near us.

Sennacherib began to remind Hezekiah of all the battles he had won in the past and made the mistake of lumping the God of Israel with all the other gods he had conquered.

What was the people's response to the mockery in 2 Kings 18: 36, and what was King Hezekiah's command?

_____

_____

_____

_____

Sometimes it is in our best interest to not fight the enemy with our words. I am reminded here of what God often told the kings and his people of old and tells us today, "The battle belongs to the Lord."

When the King of the Assyrians came with all his threats, what does Hezekiah do in 2 Kings 19:1?

_____

_____

_____

_____

He tore his clothes and covered himself with sackcloth and went into the house of the Lord. Fasting and petitioning God during a difficult season is the wisest thing we can do. What do Eliakim, Shebna, and the senior priest say to the prophet Isaiah on King Hezekiah's behalf? (2 Kings 19:3).

_____

_____

_____

_____

What is the first thing the prophet Isaiah said to them in 2 Kings 19:6?

_____

_____

_____

_____

Do not be afraid! Though the army was massive, God was on Israel's side. And God is on your side. History tells us the Assyrian army was over 300,000 men, and 185,000 died the very next day when they tried to mock the people of the Living God. Sin comes to whisper doubt and distrust in our God. It wants to rob us of our promised land. Yet God has the victory and the plan. Sometimes the largest battle, like the battle with Hezekiah and the King of the Assyrian army, is the closest thing to us, it is for our peace.

Take a moment and read 2 Kings 19:1-7 (ESV). What are we to "lift up" at the end of verse 4 (ESV)?

_____

_____

_____

_____

Even a great king, who follows the Lord God, can have a weak moment. Hezekiah was not perfect, and neither are we. Yet Hezekiah in Hebrews means, *God gives me strength*. No matter what battle you fight, God will give you strength.

Let me say, this is your day…not of distress, of rebuke, or of disgrace. You have come to the point of birth, and you will have the strength to deliver. God promises us victory. The question is not if HE is trustworthy. The question is, will WE be found trustworthy. He will provide for you the strength you need to give birth to those dreams promised by the Lord. But first, we have to rebuild trust and unity with the Father.

What does your promised land look like? What are you believing God will accomplish?

_____

_____

_____

_____

Now, take a moment and read 2 Kings 20:1-11(ESV). What were the three things God told Hezekiah through his prophet in verse 5 (ESV)?

_____

_____

_____

_____

Remember, the battle always belongs to the Lord. He has heard your prayers, my dear friend. He has seen your tears, and behold, He says, "I will heal you."

God is restoring us to reform us. From Restoration to Reformation. Just like Hezekiah stepped into his calling and destroyed all the high places and altars of the past, God is calling us to a new day. You can trust Him…we are in our promised land, kicking out the giants who have been there long enough. This was God's promise to King Hezekiah, and it is ours today.

> *I have heard your prayers.*
> *I have seen your tears.*
> *I will heal you.*

Close in prayer.

_____

_____

_____

_____

"I have *heard* your prayer;
I have *seen* your tears.
Behold, I will *heal* you."

2 Kings 20:5 (ESV)

Personal Study

Suggested Reading: Chapter 5 in *The Beautiful Ugly Truth*.

Ask God in prayer, what lies am I believing? Pause and listen. Write down what you believe God is telling you.

_____

_____

_____

_____

Is there a lie you have been believing? Repent for agreeing with the lie and spend some time journaling about it here.

_____

_____

_____

_____

Then pray and ask God, what truth do you want me to believe?

_____

_____

_____

_____

How can I partner with unity this week?

_____

_____

_____

_____

Week 4 – The Valley for Our Identity and Legacy

Imagine

Now, I am fully aware of all the wrong that was in my marriage. The betrayal, the secrets, the bowing down to high places, and giving way to one's desires had finally been exposed. We both had issues Jesus needed to heal. Secrets and disguises are deadly, as we will learn this week. The secrets in my marriage tore at my identity like an old piece of clothing. I felt vulnerable and susceptible to the next wave of deception during this season. And even though I asked for the truth, with each new wave of revelation I would feel sad one minute and angry the next. I was grieving. I knew for God to heal our marriage, the secrets had to be brought out in the open. Yet the pain of the betrayal was in the fact that my spouse disguised our marriage like everything was alright and took it out in public for everyone to see. I wrestled with my thoughts and my identity during this season like no other season before. We discovered disguises and secrets were hard to maintain over a period of time. Eventually, the truth would make its way to the surface, but not without these disguises affecting the life and breath of the marriage.

In order to rebuild trust, we must go through the process of bringing the secrets to the light. This is when we find ourselves at another crossroads. Do we do the work it takes to rebuild something broken, or do we move on, taking our baggage to the next stop?

I remember when God spoke to my heart and told me I needed to bring the weight of our broken relationship and place it on Him. He gently spoke to me and said, *I had leaned on my husband, my children, my work, and myself long enough.* It was time for me to 'lean' back on Him. He was the one who was able to handle the weight of our brokenness. God was not only healing Mark and our marriage, but He was healing me.

What is something you have leaned on long enough that God wants you to place on Him? Please write it below.

_____

_____

_____

_____

Patterns are pointers, and our feelings follow our thoughts. When my husband and I were going through our time of counseling and all the upheaval, our feelings were raw and vulnerable. I was dealing with anxiety, heartbreak, and an unsureness about myself. Mark was dealing with the shame and embarrassment of his decisions, as well as coming to an understanding of the damage they had caused in our relationship. He was also learning how his early childhood years played a significant role in the weaknesses and patterns he had developed.

When I was dealing with the relentless feelings of anxiety, our counselor told me our feelings follow our thoughts. If we don't like how we are feeling, we have to figure out what we are thinking about. I am not sure if you have noticed, but we think about things without thinking about them.

Let's face it, our brains are always processing thoughts. Studies show we produce up to 50,000 thoughts a day, and 70% to 80% of those thoughts are negative. This translates into 40,000 negative thoughts a day that need managing and filtering. Without doing so, our mind can go on auto-pilot, and if we are left to whatever thoughts hit our consciousness, we will plummet into a downward spiral. Whether we intentionally pick our thoughts or we allow our thinking to be influenced and swayed by things contrary to what God's Word says, our feelings and our emotions will follow our thoughts. It is because of this that we have to look deeper.

Imagining is part of rebuilding trust in God and in others. And if we are in a grieving stage in any relationship (marital, family, friends), we have to imagine what God thinks and how our relationships can be restored. We also must learn to take every thought captive. We must look at our circumstances with spiritual eyes and read God's Word.

Let's look at 2 Corinthians 10:3-5. Write the verses below.

_____

_____

_____

_____

Based on the verses above, why is it so important to take every thought captive?

_____

_____

_____

_____

When we take our thoughts captive we destroy arguments and every opinion raised against the knowledge of God. In other words, we destroy negative thoughts. We must choose our thoughts and imagine rebuilding trust with others and with God.

When was the last time you spent time imagining or dreaming about something?

_____

_____

_____

_____

Now, let's look at 2 Corinthians 4:18. Why is it so important to look past our current circumstances?

_____

_____

_____

_____

Not to minimize our circumstance, but I had to realize that my current situation was transient. I needed to fix my gaze and trust in the eternal. God was busy in my broken marriage. He was healing Mark, and He was healing me. God took us through the restoration process to bring reformation, healing years of broken and destructive patterns and old ways of thinking. If we fail to look past the temporal (our current situation) into the eternal (God's plan), we could miss the best part of the reformation process. Be creative with God and imagine that God is reforming you. God is so close to you. God is showing you all the ways in which He is trustworthy. I encourage you to sit with God. Imagine good things and take every negative thought captive and make it obedient to His Word.

Today I want to introduce you to the next king we will study, King Josiah.

Israel was a mess, much like my marriage. Israel was broken and split apart. After King Solomon's kingship was ripped from him, Israel was split into two kingdoms. The Northern Kingdom was ruled by King Jeroboam, and the Southern Kingdom was ruled by King Rehoboam. So much evil was done in the sight of the Lord during this time. There was the rise and fall of good kings and evil kings. High places destroyed and high places re-built. Worshiping God and worshiping idols. Trusting in a Holy God and distrusting a Holy God. We have definitely seen patterns repeat themselves over and over again throughout this study. Idol worship, wars, and battles for land and territory can show us there was a pattern. And as we study patterns, they can point us in the right direction if we let them.

This week we will see the demise of Israel again, only to experience its rebuilding. Here is where we will meet King Josiah. Only two kings in the Southern Kingdom would reign after King Hezekiah but before King Josiah. They were Manasseh and Amon. These two kings were known as two of the worst in Israel's history before King Josiah would reign. The sad thing was, these two evil kings were in Hezekiah's bloodline. Usually, a king that preceded another king was a son of the former one. Yes, they were family. Families have a way of keeping us humble, don't they?

Now, let's learn about King Josiah.

Josiah's name literally means *healed by Yahweh* or *Jehovah heals.* He was the 16th King of Judah. After the terrible rebellion, he instituted major reform by removing high places of worship to any other gods than Yahweh.

Read 2 Kings 22. How old was King Josiah when he became king? How long did King Josiah reign?

_____

_____

_____

_____

How is King Josiah's character described in 2 Kings 22:2? What did King Josiah do?

_____

_____

_____

_____

King Josiah's most recent ancestry may have been the worst of the worse, but this king had something really special going for him. All of the kings of Judah were in King David's lineage. His mother was only mentioned once in scripture. Her name was Jedidah. She was one of the wives of King Amon who gave birth to this special son. Her name in Hebrew means *darling of Jehovah*. King Josiah, though very young, was surrounded by godly, holy hearts who helped raise him. His mother, Jedidah; Hilkiah, the priest; Shaphan, the scribe;

and Huldah, the prophetess. And probably most notable was the prophet Jeremiah, who would receive his calling as prophet to the King, when he was around sixteen years old.

What did King Josiah do in his eighteenth year of reign in 2 Kings 22: 4-5?

_____

_____

_____

_____

He began to rebuild and repair the Temple that was once again in ruins. Repairing the house (temple) of God would be no easy task. It would take dedication and work. Can you imagine the temple of old and its disarray? High places, Asherah poles, and idol worship in the Temple built by Solomon to worship God. Drapery torn, altars smashed, and flooring messy and tattered. Yet, when King Josiah was 26 years old, he commissioned the repairs and restoration of the Temple.

> *"Count the money that has been brought into the house of the*
> *Lord, which the keepers of the threshold have collected from the*
> *people. And let it be given into the hand of the workmen who have*
> *the oversight of the house of the Lord, and let them give it to the*
> *workmen who are at the house of the Lord, repairing the house."*
>
> *2 Kings 22:4-5 (ESV)*

Like King Josiah, we can find our house, our temple in disarray. Broken by bad decisions and circumstances that may or may not have been in our control. And what we once trusted in is no longer standing. Repairs can be costly and can take time, but the work is worth the outcome.

Read 2 Kings 22:8-11. What did Hilkiah, the high priest, find during the repairs?

_____

_____

_____

_____

Finding the Book of the Law or the Book of the Covenant was a treasure. Why do you think King Josiah tore his clothes in verse 11? Why was he in despair?

_____

_____

_____

_____

Tearing your clothes was a sign of mourning and grief in the Old Testament. Now it makes perfect sense why I felt like my identity was like an old piece of clothing being torn. I was grieving. We can certainly look at our surroundings and be grieved or hardened by the world, and how far the depravity has come. Mourning, fasting, and asking for His mercy has a way of getting God's attention.

Though calamity was near for the Southern Kingdom, what did God tell the prophet regarding King Josiah in 2 Kings 22: 19-20?

_____

_____

_____

_____

God promises us that He hears us when our hearts are patient and humble before the Lord, like Josiah. But what else did King Josiah do as he prayed?

_____

_____

_____

_____

When was the last time God called you to be patient, humble yourself, pray and fast for someone?

_____

_____

_____

_____

Read 2 Kings 23. King Josiah began the reform of Judah. He learned from the Book of the Law and made a covenant to the Lord to keep His commandments, testimonies, and statutes with all his heart and his soul. He learned to perform the words of this covenant that were written in this book.

What did all the people do in 2 Kings 23:3?

_____

_____

_____

_____

Not only do we read of the high places, the Asherah poles, and the shrines being destroyed, but King Josiah commanded Hilkiah, the high priest, to bring all of the idol's remains from the Temple and burn them all at the Brook Kidron. Remember in week one what we learned about the Kidron Valley? The Valley of Decision.

What can we take to our Brook Kidron to destroy as a sign of worship to God?

_____

_____

_____

_____

King Josiah would also go to the cities of Samaria, the Northern Kingdom of Israel, and the high places of Bethel and destroy everything there before returning back to Jerusalem. Remember, I mentioned in week two that there were two high places built in Dan and Bethel? This is what Josiah went after. Once the house of the Lord was clean, Josiah commanded his people to do something.

Read 2 Kings 23:21. What did the king command all his people to begin in the reformation process?

_____

_____

_____

_____

Why do you believe restoring the Passover was so important?

_____

_____

_____

_____

Looking back to Exodus, it was a time of slavery. God's people had been enslaved for over 400 years. Moses would go before the Pharaoh and ask for the children of God's release. With each denial, another plague would fall upon Egypt until the 10th plague. The Passover was a sign that God's people were "passing over" from slavery into freedom and into their land of promise. God always makes a way.

Cleaning the Temple was so important in the times of King Josiah. Ridding the Temple of high places, engraved images, false idols, and restoring the Passover was a huge part of the restoration and reformation process. Josiah brought reform to the people of God in a significant way. Reform involved temple repair, organization, and rebuilding. Maybe we don't worship actual craved images and false idols, but why would it be so important to examine our hearts when trust has been broken?

Read 1 Corinthians 6:12-19. What does God say about our body in verse 19?

_____

_____

_____

_____

Reformation begins in our temple. Reformation begins with us. Like King Josiah, it usually comes after a very dark season, and the task of repair seems insurmountable. But God! Never underestimate how critical your part is in any assignment with God. Each assignment, no matter how big or small, builds on another. Remain full of trust in a God who will see you through. He is your portion when there isn't enough. I am confident there will be more battles ahead and more valleys to cross, but God will weave each one like a tapestry and reveal its beauty.

There is an ancient proverb that says, "All sunshine and no rain makes a desert." It takes rain and sunshine, pleasure and pain, good times and bad times, victory and defeat for us to grow to our fullest potential.

Sadly, King Josiah's last battle was in a place called Megiddo, as described in 2 Chronicles 35: 20-25.

Megiddo refers to a fortification made by King Ahab (not a good king) that dominated the plain of the Jezreel valley. Ahab was a king in the Northern Kingdom years past that was taken captive eventually by the Assyrian army. Is it any wonder that Megiddo's name in Hebrews means *place of crowds*? Though a great king who brought reform to Israel, this is where King Josiah would disguise himself and go to battle in the Jezreel valley. Unfortunately, it never ends well when we disguise ourselves or we try to blend in at the places of the crowds. In disguise, King Josiah died in battle.

I remember praying while studying this king. I felt I could not leave the end of King Josiah's story out of this bible study, but I desperately wanted a happy ending. I want a happy ending for everyone. Yet, as you may know, not all endings are happy ones. I asked God to help me process that not all endings are happy ones and how it related to King Josiah's death. If the king was good, why did he have to die? Often there are things we will not understand on this side of heaven. God reminded me, as I was processing King Josiah's unhappy ending, of John the Baptist. Maybe God is reminding you of a story that did not end happily when you felt you were doing everything right. This is one of the biggest steps in trusting Christ. We are called to trust God even if it doesn't make sense at the time.

Please read Matthew 11:1-6 and write verse 6 below. What happens when we are not offended by God?

_____

_____

_____

_____

John, the one who leaped in his mother's womb. John, the one who declared to make straight the path of Christ. John, by birth, who is related to Christ. John, the one who had the honor to baptize Christ. John, the one who watched Jesus do the miraculous. John, the one in prison who would be beheaded by King Herod, sent a message to ask Jesus. "Are you the one who is to come, or shall we look for another?" And Jesus answered them, "Go and tell John what you hear and see: the blind receive their sight and the lame walk, lepers are cleansed and the deaf hear, and the dead are raised up, and the poor have good news preached to them. And blessed is the one who is not offended by me," (Matthew 11:3-6 ESV).

I am sometimes convinced in life that we will have an opportunity to be offended by Christ, where we will be left with more questions than answers. Yet, we are still called to trust Christ anyway. Especially, when we do not understand. Here the word "offended" in Matthew 11:6 is the same word translated "falling away" in John 16:1. Maybe things don't make sense in your world currently but take heart, my friend, God is still for you. You belong to him. The enemy of our soul would love nothing more than for us to be offended at God. And offense can lead to a falling away. Your identity is in a God who is very trustworthy. It is our identity that is forged like gold. We must trust God when we do not understand. Continue to build on your identity because it will surely impact your legacy. Our healthy identity in Christ is connected to a healthy legacy we will leave the future generations. Imagine your future. The best gift you can give your legacy is a healthy you. God is with you.

Close in prayer.

_____

_____

_____

_____

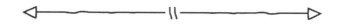

"For the creation waits with *eager longing* for the revealing of the sons [and daughters] of God."

Romans 8:19 (ESV)

Personal Study

Suggested Reading: Chapter 6 in *The Beautiful Ugly Truth*.

What perception of God needs to be healed in you?

_____

_____

_____

_____

Have you ever been offended by God? Tell Him about it here.

_____

_____

_____

_____

Imagine what your future holds. How can you partner with God, like King Josiah did to bring reformation?

_____

_____

_____

_____

Week 5 – The Valley of Transformation

Listen

Each week, we have studied some notable kings, the battles they fought, and the valleys they conquered. In rebuilding trust with God and others, these are the places we must travel to in the healing process. Listening to God's instruction and meditating on His word will only make your way prosperous. We are entering our valley of transformation.

Discovering our identity and rebuilding trust in God after a betrayal is a process. And the process is critical for not only us, but for our future legacy. Entering into our rightful place depends on it.

It seems the older we get, the more things we accumulate, including titles. I collected titles to show people who I was. Some of the titles were and are a real honor for me, while others described what I did. I was a wife, a mom, a pastor's wife, an interior designer, bible study teacher, and an account executive. There were other titles I have been associated with over the years, but as I grew older or jobs changed, some previous titles didn't seem as important as they once had.

I remember working through our betrayal when everything was shaken. I just wanted to know what happened to the person I used to be. I was changing, and I felt uncomfortable in the transformation. Often I cried, asking God what had happened to me. Who was I? I had worked so hard growing up and thought I knew. Yet, during this season, I felt so lost again. I was really unsure of myself. I desperately wanted to be heard and cared for. I wanted someone to understand my quiet suffering.

If you have read my story, you know I grew up in a broken family. The title I was least associated with was "daughter." I knew I was a daughter before all these other titles, but time, broken relationships, and distance allowed me to push this specific title further down the identity chart. Yet God was showing me it was the very thing I needed to understand so I could build my confidence again in Him. I was God's daughter. Often our perception of God is skewed because of our perception of our earthly father. Because of rejection, disappointment, and betrayal, it was like my heart was orphaned. I made inner vows and fortified every wall around my heart. "I've got this" and "I don't need anybody" were sentences that often revealed my lack of trust in others, but especially in God. Yet in this season, God was showing me how He had adopted me and how I was valuable to Him, and He had the plan. I was learning I was safe with Him on this journey of transformation. Not only was He teaching me through His word, I felt like He was listening to my cry.

"For you did not receive the spirit of slavery to fall back into fear,
but you have received the Spirit of adoption as sons, by whom we
cry, "Abba! Father!" The Spirit himself bears witness with our spirit
that we are children of God, and if children, then heirs—heirs
of God and fellows heirs with Christ, provided we suffer with
him in order that we may also be glorified with him."

Romans 8:15-17 (ESV)

I learned these trials actually become our teachers showing us how our souls can be transformed into something so much more beautiful. God was using the soil of grief in this season to allow the seeds of purpose and destiny to grow in me. It took time and seeking Him, but the further down the road I traveled with God, the more I was being transformed. There were days I didn't want to listen to anyone, but I finally learned if I wanted to be heard, I must learn to listen. I didn't want to be mad anymore. I wanted to forgive and drop the weight of unforgiveness and stretch into the warrior that was always inside of me. I wanted to trust again. Yet my reality at the time was not pretty, and neither was the transformation. It truly was a 'wrestle.' I was emerging, not as a frightened little orphan anymore, but as someone who was being fully awakened. **The darkest part of the journey thus far was proving**

to be what caused the most expansion of growth in me. My situation for a while was still the same, but something was changing inside of me. I was being made whole through all the chaos that surrounded me. Being God's daughter was about my identity. But not just mine. It was about our legacy and their identity. Would I give my children a healthy version of who God was? Your healthy identity in Christ will help produce a legacy in your life for generational blessings to come. Who I was in the big picture was larger than me. And who you are will be larger than you.

Nevertheless, I couldn't explain it all at the time, I just couldn't wait to get older when I was younger. I faced many trials growing up and I couldn't wait to make it through this trial either. I was thinking if I could just get to the next season, there would be fulfilled promises waiting. Don't get me wrong, I discovered each season had blessings, but it just seemed to take so long. As I mentioned before, I thought my promised land of purpose and destiny was a place I was going to. I had not yet realized I was already in the place of my promise all along.

You, too, are in your promised land. When we accept Christ as our Savior, we enter into our Promise and transformation begins. Our Promise is somewhere we have entered and are being transformed. Like the Israelites in Canaan, we get to kick out the inhabitants who once resided there. Seeing this truth and understanding my identity gave me the strength I needed to embrace the beauty of each moment. All the while, God was drawing me nearer. I didn't realize God would use the conflict and people to bring me peace and settle things in my heart. Jesus is good at speaking peace in the storms of life.

What does your promised land look like? Are there giants that need to be kicked out?

_____

_____

_____

_____

Walter Brueggemann is an American Protestant Old Testament scholar and theologian who is widely considered one of the most influential Old Testament scholars of the last several decades. He is an author of over one hundred books. During one of his interviews about injustice and grief in life, he said, "the Psalms and Lamentations are all an expression of grief, but they are also an expression of hope. Such prayers are partly an address to God, but they are also a communal resolve to hand in and take transformative action. Unless that kind of grief is put into speech, it will never become energy." He describes grief and injustice as a part of our life here on earth. How we respond to grief and injustice is the energy we put out into this world. From the deepest grief, we are being transformed, and from transformation, we can release our voice and hope to others. Based on the bestseller, *The Message of the Psalms*, by Walter Bresggemann, he describes this process of transformation as *orientation*, *disorientation*, and *reorientation*.

>**Orientation:** our life is one way.
>**Disorientation:** grief and injustice happens.
>**Reorientation:** transformation.

We read about this process all through the Psalms with King David.

We have studied some incredible kings thus far, but today, we are going back to go forward. Maybe this king is one of the most notable because this king knew something about rejection, conflict, betrayal, kingdoms, and the process of staying faithful…somewhat. Let me re-introduce you to King David. We all know David was a good king for Israel. Despite his glaring flaws, David is described as a man after God's own heart, but his story begins on the back side of the desert as one of the sons of Jesse. King Saul was the first King of Israel and had been rejected for not obeying God's commands. Something happened to Saul.

What happened to King Saul in 1 Samuel 15: 23b and 1 Samuel 16:14?

_____

_____

_____

_____

Because Saul had rejected the Word of the Lord and served other deities along with God, God had rejected Saul as king. The prophet Samuel followed God's direction to anoint another king of Israel as he grieved King Saul. Scripture says Samuel did not go back to see Saul after he anointed David as king. Days turned into months, and months turned into years as David himself was being transformed. He was anointed as a teenager, faced Goliath, was banished by Saul, hid in caves in the desert, lived on the run, and fought many battles. It would be 15 years from the time David was anointed until he actually became king over Israel. If anyone knew anything about rejection, grief, injustice, and being overlooked, David had ample opportunity to have a few questions. Being rejected or overlooked still feels the same today. We want to trust God, and we do…until we don't. Then all the questions arise. It was during my betrayal season when I questioned my marriage, the ministry, my relationships with others, and my relationship with God. The process of waiting and becoming is part of the battle of transformation. David was very familiar with waiting, as I am sure we all are.

What do you feel God has called you to accomplish, but you are still waiting for it?

_____

_____

_____

_____

Maybe you have read the story of how David was anointed King over Israel. Jesse had many sons. Eight to be exact. Each stood in line for the prophet Samuel to anoint the next king. But none were chosen. Samuel even asked Jesse, "Do you have another son?" Even Jesse, David's own father, didn't believe it would be David. But God said something beneficial to Samuel during the process.

What did the Lord say to Samuel in 1 Samuel 16:7? What does the Lord look at when choosing someone?

_____

_____

_____

_____

God looks at our hearts. This was not only David's season of being anointed and transformed, but it can be ours as well. I walked through many seasons of not understanding who I was in Christ. I thought I knew, but more learning, listening, and waiting came. In my deepest pain and the upheaval of my marriage, my identity and everything I knew to be true was being transformed. I learned I was more than the titles I carried; I was God's daughter. I was no longer an orphan with an orphan mentality. No longer did I need to gather titles to identify my purpose in life. I was fully accepted. I was fully adopted. I was His daughter. Broken and all.

Isn't that just like life? Our identity is forged by our life experiences.

And if we don't let pain _transform_ us, we will transmit it.

Remember, God looks at the heart. I believe God chooses us as a son or a daughter, anoints us, and then the process of becoming and being transformed begins. We are in the process of becoming. But becoming what?

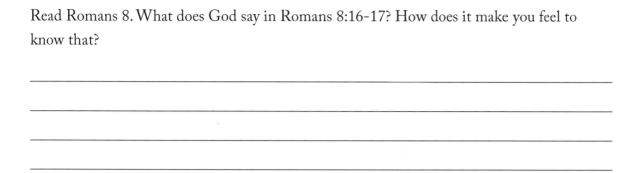

Read Romans 8. What does God say in Romans 8:16-17? How does it make you feel to know that?

_____

_____

_____

_____

Like David, we have been chosen and anointed. We are God's sons and daughters, heirs of God, and co-heirs with Christ. New Testament scriptures go on to say who we are in Christ.

"You did not choose me, but I chose you."

John 15:16a (ESV)

"who saved us and called us to a holy calling, not because of our works but because of his own purpose and grace."

2 Timothy 1:9 (ESV)

"For we know, brothers loved by God, that he has chosen you."

1 Thessalonians 1:4 (ESV)

When trust is breached, it's vital that we build a bridge in our minds through scripture to remind us of who we belong to and whose we are. David even said he would have lost hope if he had not seen the goodness of the Lord in the land of the living (Psalm 27:13-14).

Imagine for a moment being anointed King. Close your eyes. You are more than what your situation says about you currently. God has looked at your heart. He has chosen you.

As David was selected from all of his brothers, like Samuel, God calls a prophet to come find you. He has been looking for you as you have been looking for him. This speaks of the faithfulness of God and your calling. He will find you and ask for you and bring you before others. Maybe you know you have been anointed as a son or a daughter, and you are waiting and waiting. There have been many battles to this point. Maybe you have faced your fiercest giant, or you are currently facing it. I know you are familiar with the David and Goliath story, but are you familiar enough with it that you see it in your life?

Read 1 Samuel 17. What stands out to you the most in this chapter? What is your Goliath?

_____

_____

_____

_____

The Valley of Elah

The Valley of Elah is one of the most epic places and battles in scripture. It would be where David would face one of the giants of Israel, Goliath. The valley of Elah is located in a region called Shephelah. The word Shephelah comes from the Hebrew root word to mean *low, humiliated and even dejected*. In this humiliated, dejected place is actually where David would meet Goliath. God was transforming David into a King. We remember in the story how Goliath would mock and even humiliate the Israelites before David showed up.

In the valley, we face decisions, and in the valley, we face our giants. Yet in the valley, even though I know it will produce good fruit for you and me, the valley is not someplace I am really fond of. This is where my trust in God and in others can feel shaky. The valley is when we can make assumptions about God, our relationships, and who we are in Christ. The giants we face, like Goliath, can seem out of balance. Goliath was much taller than David and very intimidating and David was considered just a youth. Goliath came to threaten the freedom of Israel, and our Goliath does the same to us. Goliath's name actually means *Exposer* and *Exile*. This giant in our promised land wants to expose us, intimidate us, humiliate us, and cause us to run into exile. Yet our identity and transformation call us to move forward, to pursue. Forty days the battle waged between the Israelites and the Philistines before David even showed up.

On our way to battle, besides Goliath, who else will we meet, and what do they do? Read 1 Samuel 17:28-29.

_____

_____

_____

_____

What was David's response to his brother?

_____

_____

_____

_____

"What have I done now?" Can you hear this in David's voice? Can you hear this in your own head? Have you ever been exhausted by the people close to you? You are in good company.

Sometimes family or people close to us do not always understand what God has equipped or called us to. It is in the valley when we must lean on God and trust Him more. God is trustworthy. He is unchangeable. He believes in you and me.

Re-read 1 Samuel 17:47 again. What did David say to the Philistines? Who does the battle belong to?

_____

_____

_____

_____

The Valley of Elah would be one of many battles before David became King of Israel. While waiting, he ran for his life many times to escape the jealousy of Saul. He won multiple battles and refused to kill Saul even when given the opportunity (1 Samuel 24). We must decide to do the same when we are betrayed, rejected, and even humiliated.

We will have opportunities to take revenge or be tempted to take revenge but remember, God looks at the heart of man. What will be the energy and the outcome of our transformation? This season of grief is transforming us into someone greater than we could have ever imagined. Our rightful place is determined in the battles we face and the giants we slay. It's not about revenge; it's about releasing hope. This battle is for our identity and legacy and us stepping into our rightful place. God has called us His sons and daughters so we can walk in our calling as kings and priests. Not only does walking into our identity bless others, but it sets up our legacy for generational blessings. Becoming glorifies the Father.

Read 1 Peter 2:9. What has God called you? And what has God called you out of?

_____

_____

_____

_____

Read Revelations 1:5-6. What has God freed us from? And what has God made us?

_____

_____

_____

_____

Broken trust and valleys are leading you somewhere remarkable. We can rebuild trust in God and in the process become transformed.

You have been awakened. You are the transformation of God's glory to this world. Your trust is being fortified. You can trust God when all else fails. He will not fail you. You are in the right place.

Close in prayer.

_____

_____

_____

_____

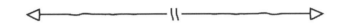

"But you are the ones *chosen* by God, chosen for the high calling of priestly work, chosen to be a *holy* people, God's instruments to do his work and speak out for him, to tell others of the night-and-day difference he made for you—from nothing to something, from rejected to accepted."

1 Peter 2:9-10 (MSG)

Personal Study

Suggested Reading: Chapter 7 in *The Beautiful Ugly Truth*.

What desire has God placed in your heart?

_____

_____

_____

_____

What is your next step?

_____

_____

_____

_____

What does leaving a legacy mean to you?

_____

_____

_____

_____

Week 6 – The Valley Shall Be Raised Up

Decide

Can you believe it? We are heading into our last week together. I wish I was sitting with you. I can picture you all together, becoming warriors, rebuilding trust. I remember walking through this study with my first group. I love those ladies. Each person, whom I can personally call by name, holds a special place in my heart. We studied hard together. We cried together. We worshiped together. And we discovered the courage to be vulnerable together. I pray you have had the same experience with your group. As we prepare to close this study until the next time, I leave you with this…

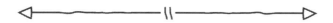

"And let us not grow weary of doing *good,* for in due season we will *reap,* if we do not give up."

Galatians 6:9 (ESV)

We cannot give up! Let us not grow weary means *do not lose heart, grow weary, relax your courage or faint.* When betrayal is a part of our lives, our trust can erode like snow on a warm day. Little by little the enemy tries to convince us that God is not good and He is not trustworthy. This lie could not be farther than the truth. Remember, betrayal can take on many forms. The enemy knows our personal kryptonite and does his best to trip us up daily. If only we could see what is really going on in the celestial world. Fortunately, we have God's Word as a road map for rebuilding trust. We were created to connect; connect with God and connect with others. God was the One to put it in our hearts to love. Love causes us to bond emotionally. Love is our bulwark (a defensive wall), providing emotional protection from life's storms. God never said we would not experience storms in life; He just promised He would be with us through them. We thrive in deep, meaningful relationships. We thrive in trust. We must not relax our courage when storms arise but look for love in the process.

Read Mark 4:35-41 in the Message translation. Describe what happened to the wind after Jesus was awakened and told the wind to, "Be Quiet! Settle Down!"

_____

_____

_____

_____

During the storms in our lives, I am so grateful for Christ, who speaks peace to the storm and causes the winds to lose their breath.

Loving one another is God's greatest command. Read Mark 12:30. Is it hard for you to love others sometimes? When is it the hardest?

_____

_____

_____

_____

Yet love comes at a price, doesn't it? And betrayal costs us more than we would probably like to pay. Thankfully, the King we will talk about today paid the ultimate debt on our behalf. King Jesus.

John Bowlby, a British Psychiatrist in the early 1900's, worked with children who were under-connected emotionally. By 1944, Bowlby published the very first paper on family therapy, *Forty-Four Juvenile Thieves*, in which he noted that "behind the mask of indifference is bottomless misery and behind apparent callousness is despair." He studied children in the 1940s who became emotionally paralyzed and craved emotional attention. If they were orphaned or if there were long stints in hospitals where parents were not allowed to be, Bowlby noticed an emotional starvation. If love is not fostered, early childhood isolation produces emotional starvation. Loving, emotional contact is as important as physical nutrition. Though Bowlby was ridiculed for the "Attachment Theory" studies, many decades and many studies later have revealed responding with empathy and care to others is a key part of emotional and spiritual wholeness. Feeling emotionally orphaned as a child or feeling left without care can cause long-term negative effects.

When we feel safe, we reach for a loved one and ask for what we need. When we feel disconnected, we demand or try to control our environment.

Why is this information so important to this study? Because at our core, we need to know we are loved. And we are loved. We are connected to someone. Jesus loves us. He runs towards us, not away, even when we feel most alone. He is our good, loving King who is trustworthy. We can reach out to him.

Distress in any relationship affects our immune system, hormones, stress levels, and our ability to heal. Underneath the distress, we ask each other...

Can I count on you? Can I depend on you? Will you be there for me? Will you respond when I need you? Do I matter to you? Am I valued and accepted by you?

When we are emotionally vulnerable, our 'built-in alarm system' goes into survival mode. The amygdala in our brain triggers an automatic response of freeze, fear or flight. It is in this moment when we don't think, and our emotions take over. We actually just feel and act. When trust is violated, it can trigger memories from our past that usually stems all the way back into our childhood, if not healed. Yet as we rebuild trust in God and reconnect with others we love, we will balance out each other's emotional equilibrium. Healing, forgiving, and building highways of trust from our brokenness means we desire to connect and walk in good health. God has a plan for you. From the beginning, God was defining and designing a redemptive plan.

From Eden, the beautiful garden, and God's divine presence evident, to Baal and the crumble of man, God sought relationship. Contrary to the perfect garden and God's divine presence, evil would offer man the option to be like God. Sin and the presence of a Holy God are opposites. God knew they could not co-exist. So He would need to make another way. The people's desire to reach the heavens in their own strength would be turned into rubble because there has never been, nor will there be, another God like our Yahweh (Genesis 11:1-9).

Read Genesis 11:1-9. What happened in these verses? Why was it so significant?

_____

_____

_____

_____

In our own strength, we cannot fix what is broken. The people of Baal desired to make a name for themselves. Some translations in scripture say, "Let us make a 'famous' name for ourselves." The tower of Babel would be erected. Babel is derived from the root word meaning *to confuse*. The building project symbolized the pride and arrogance of humans who were trying to be equal with God and not waiting on His provision. The story of the tower of Babel was to emphasize the contrast between man's strength of opinion and his own achievements versus God's intervention. Captivity would be certain.

How often in our own desire to make a name for ourselves or be right in our marriages, jobs, or families, do we fail to progress? It is then that our efforts are "confused."

Out of captivity, Moses would then lead the first exodus with God's people out of slavery and back into freedom. God's presence and the covenant of the law were birthed during this time. God reached out again to us. Yet, a golden calf representing a high place was produced while the Israelites waited for God and Moses.

Waiting on God for our due season is also a lesson in trust. Forty years into an eleven-day journey left the Israelites murmuring and complaining for a king. And a generation never entered God's rest in the promised land.

What lesson can we learn from trying to "fix" our situation with our own ideas or our own strength?

_____

_____

_____

_____

What lessons do we learn from complaining?

_____

_____

_____

_____

The Old Testament scriptures point us to Israel crying out for a king. Battles were for territory and so much more. The conflict between the powers of darkness and the presence of Yahweh was an ever-present part of life for the ancient Israelites. Remember I said patterns are pointers.

Israel enjoyed a united monarchy. The 12 tribes were under one king through the reign of Saul, David, and Solomon. **Israel's demand for a king was not just for a king, but rather the rejection of trust in Yahweh's ability to fight for Israel and their protection.** "Make us a king like other nations," (1 Samuel 8:5).

Read 1 Samuel 8:5. What were the reasons the Israelites told the prophet Samuel that they wanted a king like all the other nations?

_____

_____

_____

_____

We can come up with all kinds of reasonable thinking about why we "need" to be like others, but God knows the heart behind all our reasoning.

Who were they really rejecting in 1 Samuel 8:7?

_____

_____

_____

_____

How often do we reject God from being King over our lives? God would relent, giving Israel what they prayed for, and under Saul's reign, Israel would watch its own destruction again. God tried to warn the Israelites through the prophet Samuel, but they still wanted a king instead of trusting in God. As we learned last week, eventually, David would be chosen specifically by God. "A man after God's own heart," handpicked for the task of turning man's hearts back to God and his family. With the victory over Goliath, God would declare David's descendants' heirs of the kingship.

Christ (Yahweh) would be born through King David's lineage. Solomon would reign after David but once Solomon was gone, Israel would split into two kingdoms. It would only be a matter of time before each kingdom would fall into idolatrous disloyalty to Yahweh, as we have studied. The Northern Kingdom's fall happened almost immediately. Ten tribes were now under the dominion of other gods, and most of Israel was in exile.

During this study, we have mainly studied the Southern Kingdom, the smallest of kingdoms, and its kings. Still, we watched how "good" kings would do away with idol worship and destroy the high places and how other "not so good" kings, would turn from trusting God and rebuild idols of old. Trust would erode again and again, and eventually, the Southern Kingdom would collapse, and the people were also back in exile. Yet God, all knowing, had a plan all along. He would redeem mankind. Would we rebuild trust in Him and trust His timing?

Are there places in your life God might be pointing out to you where you do not trust His timing? What happened?

_____

_____

_____

_____

We have the benefit of hindsight now. Yet, if we do not trust God, we pause here with more questions about God and His goodness in our lives. Will we trust His goodness and His love for us? We must let Him reign on the throne of our hearts even when we don't understand. Like Israel regarding the kings of old, **when we begin to question God's love and provision for us, we look for people, possessions, and other promises to protect us.** God was making a way for Yahweh to come.

During King Josiah's reign, just before the fall of the Southern Kingdom, we learned God raised up the prophet, Jeremiah. He would be the prophet, God's voice, that would speak while all of Israel would be in exile. It would be Jeremiah's prophetic words leading us to the last king we will study.

Read Jeremiah 31:31-34 (ESV). What type of people will know the Lord in verse 34 and what will the Lord forgive?

_____

_____

_____

_____

God would make a new covenant with the WHOLE house of Israel (the Northern Kingdom) and Judah (the Southern Kingdom) from the least of them to the greatest. His covenant would be, "I will be their God, and they shall be my people." The new covenant would be a promise of redemption by God to people as individuals rather than as a nation. And this new covenant would be on the basis of God's grace rather than a person's adherence to the law. God would forgive sin and restore fellowship with those whose hearts are turned towards Him. And Christ would die on a cross so that God would remember our sins no more.

Yahweh, King Jesus, would come as a baby wrapped in clothes unrecognizable as a King. God provided a way for His family to be whole again. No longer His presence in a box. His presence would become palpable. Born of a virgin, raised to life to set us free from betrayal and our lack of trust, die for our sins and allow us all to be born to new life. The Almighty God, the King of all Kings, took off deity and came as a little baby.

I am convinced God is a bit of a mystery. This is why rebuilding trust in Him is so valuable.

Solomon wished for wisdom and penned the Proverbs. Please read Proverbs 3 and then return to Proverbs 3:5-8. What stands out most to you?

_____

_____

_____

_____

Rebuilding trust in God means we cannot lean on our own understanding. Trust means *a firm belief in the reliability, truth, ability, or strength of someone*. Yahweh and His redemption was the only way. If the enemy only knew Yahweh would be born as a baby, sit before Pharisees to teach as a teenager, grow into a man, gather disciples, perform miracles, be hated by religious leaders, then die a cruel death for mankind…for us…for you, maybe the mystery of redemption and resurrection would have been spoiled.

Christ became bound up for us so we could become free. Throughout the centuries and all of mankind, God has been revealing Himself. I am sure your story has all kinds of twists and turns, too, yet when hindsight is applied to parts of our lives, we can see God's redemption and timing were as personal to us as it was to the Israelites.

I remember when God was healing my broken heart. Mark and I were in counseling. Most days, I had little to no energy. The emotional energy to move forward was exhausting. It was difficult to put a smile on my face and one foot in front of the other some days. Yet one particular day, I had made my way to the beach. We lived in Florida at the time. I was afraid and broken. I was exhausted by my relentless thoughts and questions. I felt fragile and defensive. I did not like the way those feelings felt.

I was hoping and believing this day, the ocean and the people watching would be a distraction from my circumstances. With the ocean in sight and the sand at my feet, listening to the waves brought a sense of God's peace and presence. Deep emotional healing was taking place, and I was somewhat unaware. I remember God asking me, "What are you so afraid of?" I quickly responded in thought, *I am afraid of being alone and I am afraid I will break*. I am not 100% sure how this conversation happened and how it continued onward for the next forty-five minutes. I knew my feet were in the sand, but my mind was transported somewhere else.

When I told God I was afraid I would break, I pictured a clear, glass ornament falling to the ground. I knew it represented me, and if this ornament hit the ground, shattering would be the outcome. The ornament was thin and looked so fragile, just like my heart. As soon as I saw the ornament falling, I saw God's hand reach under it for its safe landing. His hand reached under the ornament, caught it from shattering, and He held it tenderly. My heart felt safe. I remember Him telling me, "You are never alone, and I will not let you break."

It was great reassurance for the journey ahead. He was letting me know in all our upheaval, He would prove Himself trustworthy. Little did I know that day, I was going through my own counseling session. This emotional counseling session continued in my mind as He brought to mind some of my most traumatic memories in my past to reframe them. One by one, a childhood memory would vividly appear in my mind as I walked alone. I instinctively wanted to turn away from these memories. I really didn't want to remember the pain I had survived in the past. Yet with each memory, He would beckon me to come near and look again. As I returned to the memory only in my mind, He would ask me, "Where do you see me in this memory?" As I looked back into each of these scenes, once leaving its mark on my young life, I saw myself sitting in His lap. Another scene I was running into His arms, and yet another scene I watched as He protected and defended me. He was reframing these emotional, traumatic memories. And in these moments, I learned He was always with me, even when I believed I was alone and afraid. He was providing me a safe place to heal.

Now, let's look at Hebrews 13:5. What stands out to you in this verse?

_____

_____

_____

_____

I will never leave you nor forsake you is what stands out to me. These are two words we must study. The Greek word for "leave" is *aniemi*. This word means, *I will never…send back, let go, relax, loosen, give up or desist from.* **He will not leave you.**

The second word, "forsake" is the Greek word *egkataleipo*. This word means to *leave behind, to abandon, or to desert.* God is saying that He will never send you back, let go of you, relax or loosen His grip on you, leave behind, abandon, or desert you. In a world changing and where people can just walk away, God promises us He won't. This promise is also the promise God gave Joshua before entering the promised land.

Let's read Deuteronomy 31:1-8. Please write down Deuteronomy 31:8 as a promise from His word to you. What promises did God tell the people of Israel and Joshua in verse 6 and verse 8 that are the same in Hebrews 13?

_____

_____

_____

_____

As we journey further into our promised land, we must know that no matter the current situation, God is in you and for you. He will never leave you nor forsake you. When all else fails, you can trust in a living God.

Like in the Garden of Eden, God knew He could no longer walk "among" us. Sin changed things. Nor could He any longer "tabernacle" with us, like in the Holy of Holies, where priests were only allowed to meet with Him once a year. Oh no, God wanted more. God desired a family.

God knew He had to be "in" us. So He sent His Son, a trustworthy King to be our advocate. And when we accept this gift of salvation, He becomes part of us. This is why He can never abandon, desert us or relax His hold on you. He is in you.

How reckless of God. Not in character but reckless in His love for us. To send His beloved Son to take the place of all sin, to call us family, and to make us whole. No doubt, free will and sin pains the father's heart. I heard a worship leader say, "Seventy times seven is a lot of times to get your heart broken." And even though Jesus told Peter to forgive that many times, it is not a pass for us after we reach seventy times seven. He just meant there would be no limits to God's forgiveness. What great news.

Yet, I will be honest. It's difficult for me to forgive seven times. So God sent His Son so we could experience His love, real love and real connection. Yahweh came to fight for you. You are worth it. Forgiveness unlocks the power of God in our lives and will be a part of our healing. Rebuilding trust in God will build your faith and understanding. I mentioned in the last chapter of my book that we do not take territory back when we try to fight the enemy. He is already a defeated foe. **We take territory back when we believe, when we forgive, when we rebuild trust after betrayal.**

Rebuilding trust with others is possible when we rebuild trust in the One who will not relax His hold on us. Our trust must be restored vertically so we can venture to rebuild our trust with others horizontally. Remember when our counselor told me, "Until you trust Mark, you trust God in Mark." Rebuilding trust in others must start with God first. All roads lead to God. He is our King worthy of our trust.

Lastly, we look at the journey we might travel and the enemies we might encounter to enter the promised land God has destined for you and me.

Let's read Exodus 23:20-33. Describe below the enemies the angel would lead Israel to on their way to their promised land in verse 23.

In many commentaries, "the angel" referenced in verse 23 was Jesus Christ before He was incarnate.

What instructions did the angel give God's people in Exodus 23:23-25?

_____

_____

_____

_____

"You shall not bow down to their gods nor serve them, nor do as they do, but you shall utterly overthrow them and break their pillars in pieces. You shall serve the Lord your God, and He will bless your bread and your water and I will take sickness away from among you," (Exodus 23:24-25).

In studying each of these tribes, it was interesting what each of their names meant.

> The Amorites mean *bitterness, rebellion, and judging.*
> The Hittites mean *one who is broken, who fears, discouragement.*
> The Perizzites mean *rejected urban living, living in open country, not protected by city walls. Typically did not follow authority, false security.*
> The Hivites, most likely a branch of the Hitites, mean *one who is broken, terror, fear.*
> The Canaanites mean in Hebrew *to be brought down by heavy load.* They were considered lowland people, peddlers, traders, and merchandisers.
> The Jebusites mean to *trample, pride and elevation.* The Jebusites like to puff up and trample others.

Each of these nations was considered stronger than the Israelite nation, yet God told them, "I will blot them out," in verse 23.

God instructs us as we rebuild trust and enter our promised land, we must not serve any other gods of bitterness, judgment, rebellion, fear, discouragement, false security, or pride. As our trust grows, God promises we will increase and possess the land.

How did the Lord promise to drive the enemies out in Exodus 23:30?

_____

_____

_____

_____

When did God say you would possess the land?

_____

_____

_____

_____

Little by little God will drive our enemy out before you, until we increase and possess the land. Don't ever be discouraged by the process. God is moving in your journey. You will possess the land as you increase with God. I wish I could give you a hug and tell you what a great job you have done.

> Rebuilding trust in God is healing.
> Rebuilding trust in God defines us.

As we seek first God's kingdom, all these other things will work themselves out. Rebuild trust my friend. God is making all things beautiful in its time.

Close in prayer.

_____

_____

_____

_____

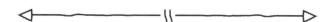

All at once the wind stopped howling and the water became perfectly *calm*. Then he turned to his disciples and said to them, "Why are you so afraid? Haven't you learned to *trust* yet?"

Mark 4:39-40 (TPT)

Personal Study

Suggested Reading: Chapter 8 in *The Beautiful Ugly Truth*.

What is God showing you again and again?

_____

_____

_____

_____

What is God reconnecting in your lives right now?

_____

_____

_____

_____

About Reconnecting Lives Ministries

Gwen Brague is co-founder of Reconnecting Lives Ministries with her husband and pastor, Mark Brague. Their home and ministry is located in Atlanta, Georgia. RLM exists to be a friend of couples and marriages new and old. Whether you are just getting starting in marriage or have years of experience, our team will walk by your side to encourage you along your journey back to health in your marriage through:

- marriage coaching
- books and resources
- bible studies
- zoom chats
- daily devotions

For more information about
Reconnecting Lives Ministries, visit
www.reconnectinglives.org

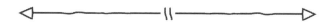

About *The Beautiful Ugly Truth* Book

What do you do when secrets and brokenness in your marriage are being exposed, and your spouse is the pastor?

More and more, we are hearing of pastors and their marriages crumbling under the weight of deception stemming from betrayal and secrets kept. Once secrets are exposed, we begin to question what we believed about the pastor, the marriage, about God and the people who surrounded us. We even question our own intuition as our heart shatters. It is a season when there are more questions than answers.

This is a pastor wife's candid journey through the recovery of a marriage and a ministry broken by secrets, betrayal, and pornography. You are not alone. Statistics say over 21 million women suffer from betrayal trauma linked to infidelity. And an estimated 40 million Americans regularly visit internet pornography sites on a regular basis. Pastors

and their wives are not immune to this forceful lure. But hope is available. Recovery is possible. Gwen invites you into her journey of faith, personal experience, and vulnerability in hopes to encourage others that God is still good. He is in your pain. And He still has a plan.

The Beautiful Ugly Truth was written for pastors and their families. It was written for couples who serve in ministry and it was also written for any marriages in need of hope during betrayal.

You will learn how to....

> Recover your life,
>
> Rebuild your identity, and
>
> Reconnect with your spouse after betrayal.

Our brokenness and what seemed to be the death of our marriage was really the birthing of something new.

Available for purchase on
Amazon.com

About the Author

Gwen Brague is a wife, a mom, a friend, bestselling author, and co-founder of Reconnecting Lives Ministries. She loves Jesus, her husband, her grown children and all kinds of God's people. She believes nothing is too hard to accomplish if you put your mind to it and is passionate about seeing hurting marriages reconnect and recapture their first love.